Prayer Is...

FURN L. KELLING

ILLUSTRATED BY RONNIE HESTER

Broadman Press
Nashville, Tennessee

4242-56
ISBN: 0-8054-4256-1

Dewey Decimal Classification: C248.3
Subject heading: PRAYER

Printed in the United States of America

Prayer is . . .
talking to God
and knowing that God is wherever I am.

Prayer is...
listening to a bird sing and thanking God
that I can hear it.
It is seeing beautiful things God has made
and thanking him.

Prayer is...
thanking God for friends
and asking God to help me be like Jesus.

Prayer is...
asking God which way is right when I don't
know. It is choosing good food to eat and
thanking God for the food.

Prayer is...
thanking God for the people who help me
have food to eat—the farmers, the grocers,
the bakers, and others.

Prayer is...
coming home to my family and thanking
God for them. It is asking God to be
near when I am afraid.

Prayer is...
asking God to help a friend who is sick.
It is thanking God for doctors and nurses
who help the sick.

Prayer is...
talking to God about other people who
need help—people who need a home or
who need friends.

Prayer is...
talking to God with my family. It is
talking to him about people who have
never heard of Jesus.

Prayer is...
asking God to help me do the things he
wants me to do. It is thanking him before
I go to bed.

Prayer is...
talking to God with all the people at
church.

Prayer is...
asking God to help me all day when I
wake up in the morning. It is telling
God I love him.

Prayer is...
thanking God for answering my prayers.
It is telling God I am sorry when
I do wrong things.

Prayer is...
thanking God for people who help us—
police, teachers, fire fighters, and
workers who deliver the mail.

Prayer is...
talking to God when someone is unkind to
me. It is asking God to help me be kind
at all times.

Prayer is...
a good feeling because God is with me.
It is knowing God loves me and is taking
care of me.